ELECTRICITY

By

Steffi Cavell-Clarke

©2017
Book Life
King's Lynn
Norfolk PE30 4LS

ISBN: 978-1-78637-159-1

Written by:
Steffi Cavell-Clarke

Edited by:
Charlie Ogden

Designed by:
Danielle Rippengill

A catalogue record for this book
is available from the British Library

CONTENTS

Words that look like **this** can be found in the glossary on page 24.

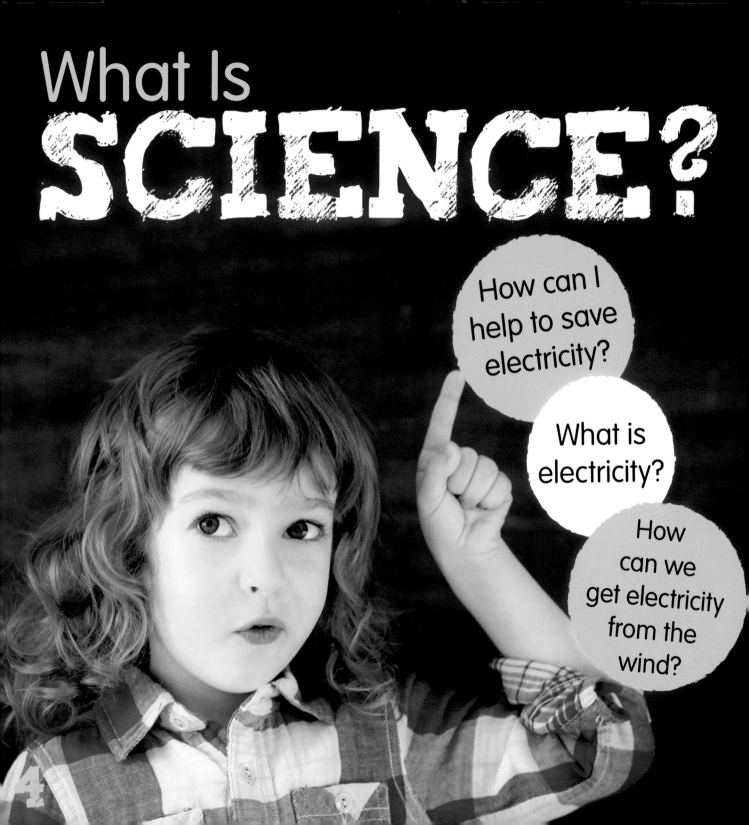

What Is SCIENCE?

How can I help to save electricity?

What is electricity?

How can we get electricity from the wind?

Science can answer many difficult questions we may have and help us to understand the world around us.

ELECTRICITY?

Electricity is a type of **energy** that gives things power.
Most people use electricity every day.

A lot of things in the home need electricity to work. The radio, the television and the telephone all need electricity to work. These things are called electrical **appliances**.

Using ELECTRICITY

Lamps use electricity to make light.

Radios use electricity to make sound.

Electrical appliances need to be plugged into **sockets** and switched on before the electricity can power them.

Sockets have a switch that turns the flow of electricity on and off. When the switch is on, electricity flows through the socket.

Never play with sockets. They can be very dangerous!

Sockets

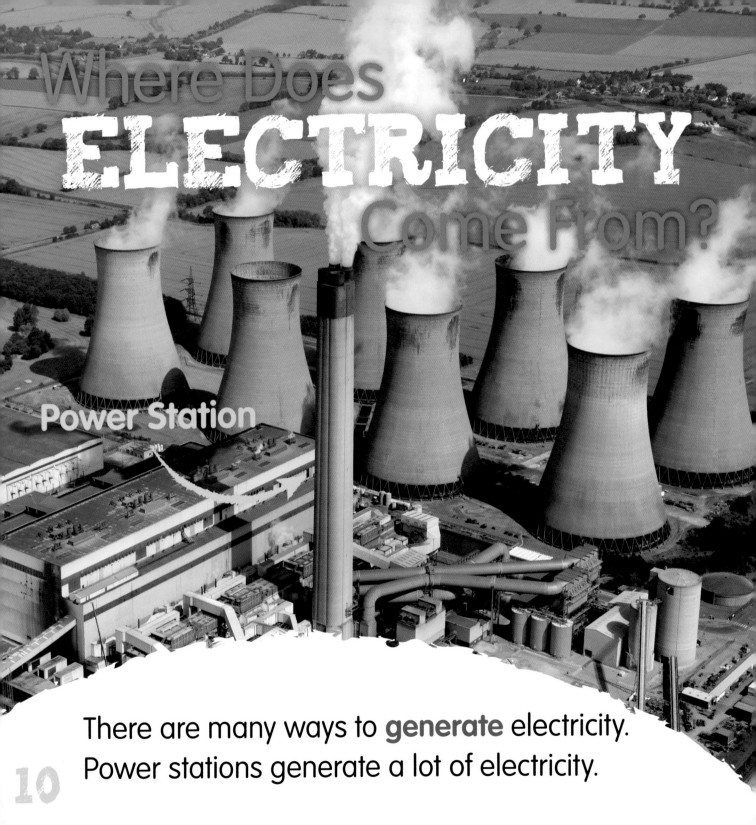

Where Does ELECTRICITY Come From?

Power Station

There are many ways to **generate** electricity.
Power stations generate a lot of electricity.

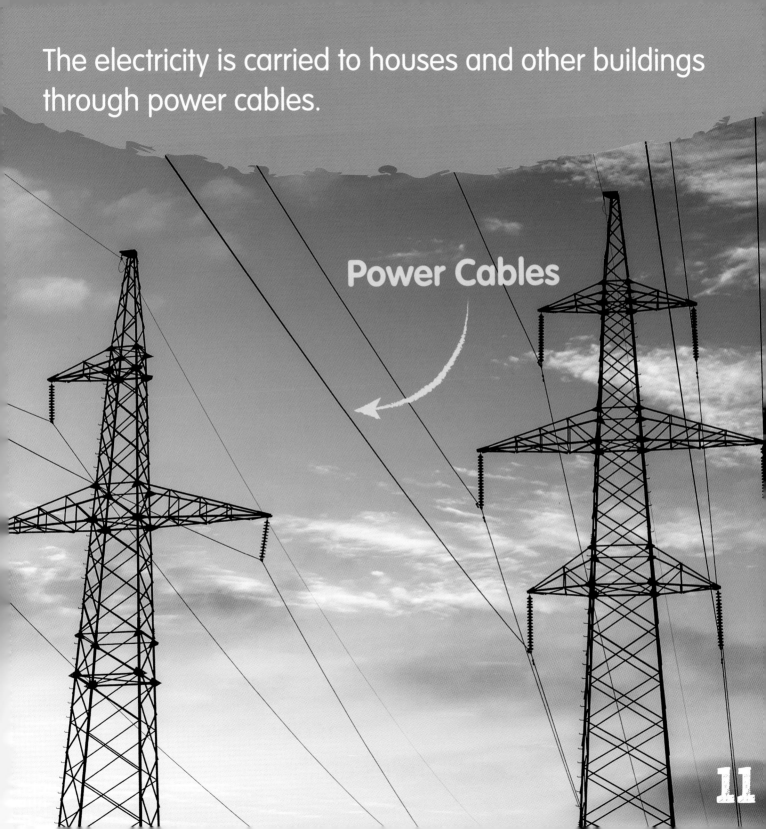

The electricity is carried to houses and other buildings through power cables.

Power Cables

Electricity from
THE WIND

Wind Turbine

Blades

Wind turbines generate electricity using the wind.
The wind turns the blades on the wind turbines.

As the blades turn in the wind, the wind turbines generate electricity.

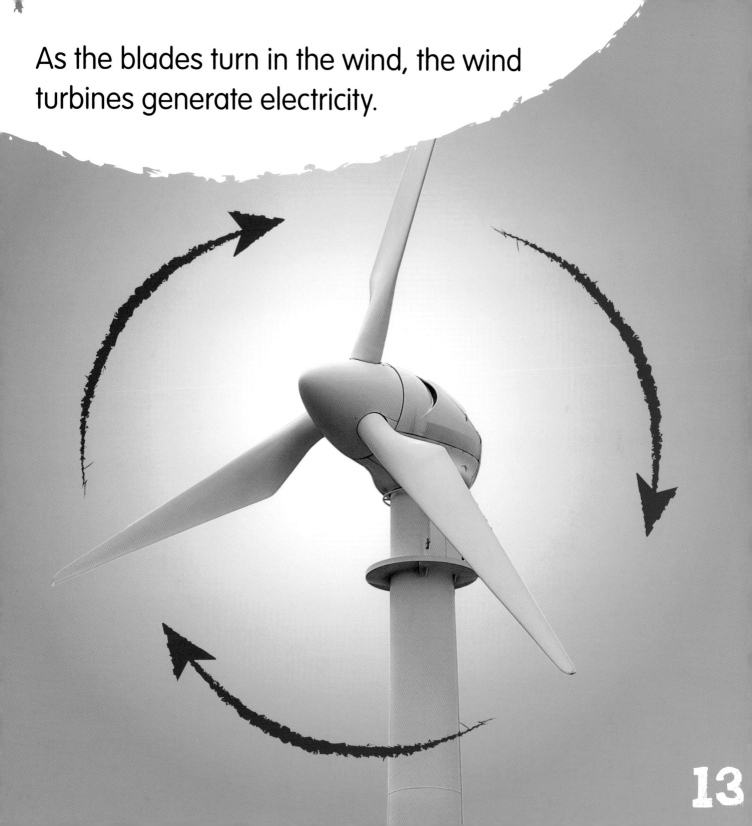

Electricity from
THE SUN

Sunlight can be used to generate electricity. This is called solar power.

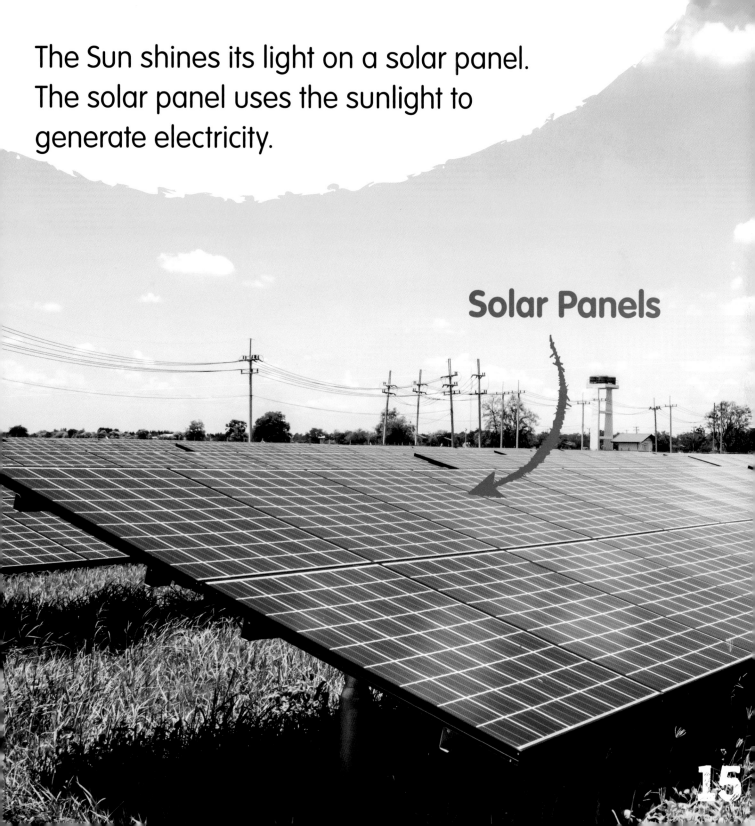

The Sun shines its light on a solar panel. The solar panel uses the sunlight to generate electricity.

Solar Panels

15

Making a
CIRCUIT

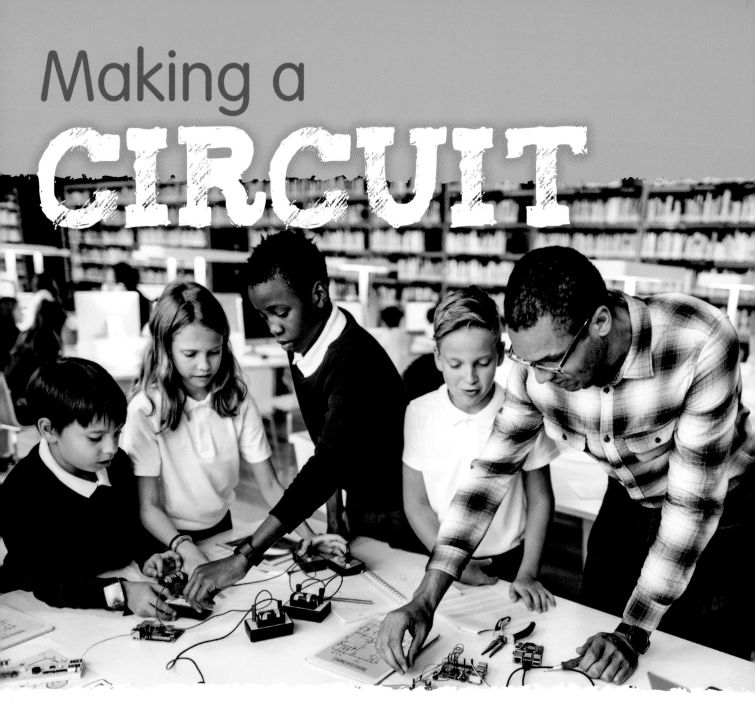

Electricity can only flow around a loop that is complete.
This loop is called a circuit.

An electrical circuit is made up of parts called **components**. The components are joined together by wires. The electricity flows through the wires and to the components.

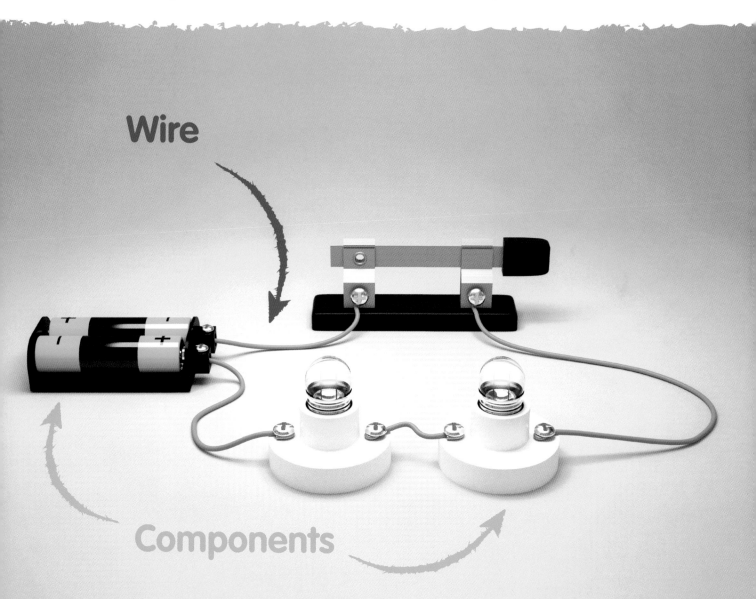

Wire

Components

Staying SAFE

Electricity can be very dangerous. It is important to always be careful when using electricity and electrical appliances.

Stay safe and remember these top safety tips:
- Never put your fingers in sockets.
- Keep metal items out of toasters.
- Never use any electrical items around water.
- Never pull a plug out of a socket by its cord.
- Do not plug lots of appliances into one socket.

Saving ELECTRICITY

It is very important to save electricity. Generating electricity can be hard and expensive, so it is important not to waste any.

Every time you turn off a light or switch off an appliance, you are saving electricity. Remember to always switch electrical appliances off when you are not using them.

Let's EXPERIMENT!

Do you know how to make a circuit? Let's find out!

YOU WILL NEED:

Crocodile clips
Plastic-coated wires
A light bulb
A light bulb holder
Batteries
A battery holder

STEP 1

Before you can light up the light bulb, you need to make a circuit. First, screw the light bulb into the light bulb holder and make sure that the batteries are safely in the battery holder.

STEP 2

Connect one end of each wire to the battery holder using the crocodile clips.

STEP 3

To complete the circuit, use the crocodile clips to connect the opposite ends of the wires to the light bulb holder.

TOP TIP:
Ask an adult to help you!

RESULTS:

Your light bulb will light up! This is because electricity can travel from the battery, along the wires, through the light bulb and back to the battery again.

23

GLOSSARY

appliances	things that can be used for a special task
components	things that do a job in a circuit
energy	power used for an activity
generate	produce or create electricity
sockets	electrical devices that hold a plug
sunlight	light from the Sun

INDEX